*Lessons Learned from
My Children about My*

# HEAVENLY
# FATHER

*Lessons Learned from
My Children about My*

# HEAVENLY
# FATHER

JON LANDS

GETHSEMANEPRESS
NASHVILLE ✡ JERUSALEM

GETHSEMANE*PRESS*
NASHVILLE ✡ JERUSALEM

*Lessons Learned from My Children about My Heavenly Father*

Library of Congress Control Number:  2018910267
Hardcover ISBN: 978-0-9854633-8-0
Paperback ISBN: 978-0-9854633-9-7
*For more resources by Jon Lands go to*
*www.TheWordForLifeRadio.com*

*Follow Jon Lands on Twitter @PastorJonLands*

Printed in the United States of America

To my children and gifts from God,

Ryan (Ryno)
Jenna (Jenna-Benna)
Maggie (Magpie)
Josiah (Jo-Jo)

*Docendo Discimus*
"Men learn while they teach."
Seneca the Younger,
Letters to Lucilius, Book I, Letter 7, Section 8

# CONTENTS

# PREFACE

I am a horrible father. I mean it—*terrible*. I hope my children would not say the same. In fact, in comparison to some men, I would win the prize as the #1 dad. However, my assessment as a terrible dad is based on the fact that I am rating my role as a father by the highest standard – my Heavenly Father.

For the past eighteen years, I have experienced the joy of hearing my children call me Daddy. It never gets old to me, although it can be a burden at times. Nothing catches my ear quicker than to hear the word, "Daddy."

Lately, though, I have noticed that the older my children grow, the more they call me "Dad" in deeper, more mature tones around their friends. But thankfully, at the end of the day, while we settle in for the evening intimacy as a family, they have no problem calling me "Daddy."

That title Daddy carries a meaning of warmth, love, and patience. The similar term in the Bible is "Abba." In the darkest hour of Christ's life in the Garden of Gethsemane, Christ cried out, "Abba Father," an Aramaic term of endearment that is closest to our term "Daddy." The phrase "Abba Father" is perhaps more closely akin to the common phrase, "Daddy, Daddy." Two times in Scripture, we are told we can call on our Father as "Abba Father," because we are his sons and daughters (Romans 8:15 and Galatians 4:6).

To call our Heavenly Father "Daddy" speaks of intimacy and affection. Our God is not a distant deity that responds with uncaring silence when we call, but a Father who welcomes us to rest on His lap so we can talk to Him privately and personally. That is my Abba Father.

Someone once wrote:

> *A daddy is someone who*
> *wants to catch you before you fall*
> *but instead picks you up,*
> *and lets you try again.*
> *A daddy is someone who*
> *wants to keep you from making mistakes*
> *but instead lets you find your own way,*

*even though his heart breaks in silence*
*when you get hurt.*
*A daddy is someone who*
*holds you when you cry,*
*scolds you when you break the rules,*
*shines with pride when you succeed,*
*and has faith in you even when you fail...*[i]

Please do not misunderstand. My children are not perfect, and I am most certainly not an impeccable dad. What is good in my relationship with my children is a reflection of the Heavenly Father's bond with His children. What is flawed in my relationship with my children as a human father reminds me to be grateful for the perfect, unspoiled grace by which our Father loves us.

Our relationship with our Heavenly Father is not fully appreciated until we can understand who He is and not just what He does for us. A blessed father is a man whose children run into his arms even when his hands are empty. Our relationship with our Heavenly Father is most robust when we run to experience the warmth of His embrace and not merely to receive the reward of His blessings.

Since our first child came into our home, I have been experiencing an education in parenthood. Every milestone in my children's life is a reminder of God's love for me as His child, and every failure as a father reminds me of the unfailing love of my Heavenly Father.

We can learn much about our Heavenly Father if we will take a moment to listen to our children. This book is a collection of lessons I learned about my Heavenly Father from my children, mined from the treasury of many mundane and a few meaningful moments. In truth, I am not a spiritual giant that God speaks to in booming tones. I am, in fact, a fragile man to whom God speaks in whispers of His Word. God wants to whisper to you too if you bend your ear to hear.

This book is not about my children, or me, but it is a guide to the reality that you can learn more about your relationship with your Heavenly Father. Take a moment and "receive the Kingdom of God as a little child" (Luke 18:17), and you too can hear the still small voice of the Spirit speaking as you listen to your children.

# CHAPTER ONE
## *Out of the Mouth of Babes*

In biblical times children seldom interacted with adults in general and were never to be heard. But Jesus turned that cultural practice on its head when He went to Jerusalem with His earthy parents to celebrate Passover months before His bar mitzvah.

When Mary and Joseph departed from the hustle and bustle of the holy days they didn't recognize Jesus was left behind in Jerusalem. A whole day later they discovered His absence.

After a frantic return and search of Jerusalem, they found the pre-teen Jesus speaking to the sages and teachers of the Temple.

Scripture records all in the Temple who heard Jesus were astonished at the understanding and answers of the twelve-year-old (Luke 2:49).

Jesus not only taught as a child; He encouraged other children to speak words of praise openly. Matthew 21:14-16 records of the time when Jesus returned to the same Temple He visited in His youth. Just after Jesus' triumphal entry into Jerusalem, He healed the lame and blind gathered at the Temple. Seeing these miracles, the children who followed Christ continued to shout "Hosanna to the Son of David!" Many of those same rabbis and religious leaders from twenty-one years earlier saw the spectacle of praise and were indignant.

With piercing conviction, Christ asked those pious leaders, most of whom were parents, if they had ever read Psalm 8:2.

"Out of the mouth of babes...thou hast perfected praise."

What Jesus was teaching the most self-righteous people of His day is a lesson we should learn as well. Children are a gift from God, and the brief journey we share with them from birth to adulthood is humbling and enlightening. Being a parent is a life lesson in the grace of our Heavenly Father towards His children.

Jesus drew this application when He asked, "If you, being evil, know how to give good gifts unto your children, how much more shall your Father which is in heaven give good things to them that ask him?" (Matthew 7:11).

Our children are often teaching us, and they don't even realize it. And if we are not paying attention, we may miss it too. As we relate to our child in the daily path we call parenthood, we learn about our Heavenly Father and how He loves us as His child, with far greater love.

# CHAPTER TWO

# The Lesson of Synergy

Late in the evening on April 24, 2000, the phone rang, and Jenny answered immediately, recognizing the number on the caller ID.

It was our adoption agency.

On the other end of the line, a social worker gave her the good news that our birth mother had delivered a healthy nine-pound baby boy and that "our son's" picture was on the way to our email.

The minutes seemed like hours while we waited for all the data packets to download and assemble a picture of our son. But it finally arrived.

There he was, *our son*, wrapped in a hospital blanket, ruddy in complexion, and amazingly, his eyes were wide open.

We already knew him, although we had never met him. He was our son—the son we had waited for, hoped for, prayed for, and for whom we even begged God. We knew his name before he was born—Jonathan Ryan Lands. Jonathan, after me, means "gift of God" and Ryan, because the name means "little king." Both names aptly describe my first-born son.

Each time I look back on that day, I remember God's promise of synergy in the lives of His saints.

*"And we know that all things work together for good to them that love God, to them who are the called according to his purpose." – Romans 8:28*

Romans 8:28 promises us that all things, good and bad, pure and evil, beautiful and ugly, easy and hard, work together. The Greek word for "work together" is the root word for our English word "synergy." Synergy is defined as this: "The whole is greater than the sum of the parts." In other words, you can do more with less.

Let me give you an example of synergy. Where I grew up, we like to go to events called tractor pulls. The floor of an arena is filled with dirt and good-ole-boys in souped-up tractors compete to see who can pull the most massive loads. In reality, tractor pulls are nothing new, because long before the internal combustion engine, farmers were competing with animals to see which one was strongest. They still have competitions in which workhorses compete.

The beautiful Clydesdale breed has always been one of the stoutest horses. Long before the Budweiser wagon, Clydesdales were pulling substantial loads. In these competitions, competitors made an exciting discovery. One horse could pull a heavy load, but when yoked with another horse, the two horses working together could pull more than the sum of the amount that each horse could pull alone.

For example, let's say a single Clydesdale can pull a sled holding two tons of weight. In addition, another Clydesdale can pull three tons. You would think that when yoked together, the most they could pull would be five tons (2+3=5). However, in reality, when these two horses are hitched together, they can pull seven tons! Two Clydesdales pulling together can accomplish more than the sum of the two parts. That is synergy!

God specializes in synergistically working through the events we wish would have never occurred. This divine synergy takes people who are considered worthless and meaningless and uses them to accomplish the greater good for His glory.

The Bible is full of examples of synergy, but the best case is of Joseph. In Genesis 50, we find Joseph serving as the governor of Egypt and quite successfully too. But if you know the backstory of Joseph, it was not an easy journey.

It all began when his resentful brothers conspired to kill him and then ended up selling him into slavery. From there, it continued to go downhill before he came to the top. Joseph was accused of rape, abandoned, and then forgotten in an Egyptian prison for years until finally, at the right time; Joseph is brought to the mind of the cupbearer of the Pharaoh as an interpreter of dreams. And as they say, the rest is history.

Now in Genesis 50, we find Joseph standing before his brothers who started all of this mess. Will he confront them for their evil deed or banish them to return to Israel to die in the famine? What can you say to someone who has done so much evil to you? Let's listen in to the conversation in Pharaoh's chamber:

> *"But as for you, you meant evil against me; but God meant it for good, in order to bring it about as it is this day, to save many people alive." – Genesis 50:20*

To Joseph, this promise was his life jacket when he was sinking in a sea of despair. He never hid the reality of evil in his life from his devious brothers. He remembered the dark pit and his torn, bloodstained coat of many colors. How could he forget Potiphar's wife's deceit and the miscarriage of justice that sent him to prison for years? Yet Joseph had seen God redeem his sorrows for sovereign good. And with that trust, Joseph's ripped robe became a royal one. His dark pit became a majestic palace. His shattered family was put back together again. The very events of his life that could have drowned Joseph turned out to strengthen him.

That is sovereign synergy! As Max Lucado so aptly put it, "In God's hands intended evil becomes eventual good."ii When Joseph told his brothers, "You meant evil against me." The Hebrew word for "meant" has a root meaning to "weave" or "braid."

God stretches our lives, like yarn, upon the loom of His sovereignty, marked by our birth and our death and having intertwined in it the pains of our sinful choices and pleasures we experience in life. He moves the shuttle back and forth across our days and even generations until His divine design appears as a tapestry of His grace.

One day, God opened the planning room of heaven to reassure Jeremiah and the exiles when He said, "For I know the thoughts that I think toward you, says the LORD, thoughts of peace and not of evil, to give you an expected end" (Jeremiah 29:11). Again God employs the visual of a cord when He used the word "expected." Later, God will give Jeremiah a remedial reminder of this promise when He says, "And there is hope in your end, says the LORD, that your children shall come again to their own border" (Jeremiah 31:17). God told Jeremiah to trust Him as He tied up the loose ends with the promise of God's goodness by the exiles return to their homeland from Babylonian Captivity.

The same Hebrew word was used when the Israelite spies in Jericho told Rahab, a prostitute, to place "a scarlet cord" in her window so she would be safe from the battle (Joshua 2:18, 21). By sparing Rahab's life, God embroidered the unexpected, which was made beautiful, in the lineage of our Lord. For the Scripture unashamedly lists Rahab the Harlot as a distant grandmother to Jesus Christ (Matthew 1:5).

Again, God is able to weave together the bad, ugly, horrid moments that cross the loom of our lives to add depth, color, and meaning to who we are for our good and ultimately His glory. That is sovereign synergy!

Looking back, it is incredible how the synergy of the Romans 8:28 promise worked together in our lives. You see, thirteen months before Ryan's birth, Jenny and I started the grueling and lengthy process of adoption. That meant four months after we applied to adopt, unknown to us and in another part of the world, our son was conceived.

That was not an accident. It was providence.

Life does not "just happen." God, in His divine design, has ordained that when life is placed in a woman's womb that this child is the fruit of the miraculous work of creation that was started in the Garden of Eden and continues in the work of procreation.

In our case, the work of procreation did not occur in the most ideal of circumstances. It was a crisis pregnancy. Our birthmother was raised in a godly home, and at sixteen, she recognized she was pregnant at her sixth month from a brutal secret she had hidden from her parents. This pregnancy was not one of her own choice, and many Christians would have advised her that this was an allowable exception for abortion. Fortunately, our birthmother's parents were strong Christians and doggedly pro-life. When they recognized the situation, they made every allowance for her to carry this child to term.

I am thankful for their pro-life stance and their willingness to stand by their daughter and support her in a crisis and ultimately counsel her toward adoption. She was blessed to stay at the Liberty Godparent Home in Lynchburg, Virginia until she delivered. There, she received the medical assistance and counsel she needed without shame or criticism.

For a birthmother to begin the process of adoption, she is asked to look through the Lifebooks of potential adoptive parents. We prepared our Lifebook approximately nine months earlier and had been losing hope with each passing month.

Jody Cantrell Dyer precisely wrote in her memoir of the adoption process, "Adoption is grief in reverse."[iii] The one thing we had heard over and over again from previous birthmothers that reviewed our Lifebook was that they didn't want their child to be raised in a preacher's home. I do not know why. Perhaps they thought we would be judgmental or unloving. But let me tell you that such an end would have been the furthest from the truth.

Thankfully, our birthmother said that the one thing she wanted above all else for Ryan was that he was to be raised in a pastor's home. Our birthmother chose us based on our Lifebook, believing God had ordained us to raise her child, not just in a Christian home, but in a *pastor's* home. She wasn't impressed by pictures of fun vacations, annual income, or educational background. She just wanted her child to be a P.K. (Preacher's Kid).

That is synergy. Just at the right time, God was able to turn a horrible circumstance for good and for His glory.

And God is not finished yet. As I look at my son, I see potential and hope as he yields his life to God. Ryan can change the world as he fulfills God's purpose for his life. I know he has certainly changed our world.

CHAPTER THREE

# *The Patience of My Father*

We were running late. Ryan and I had to be at the church for the children's Christmas program practice at 2:00 PM, and it was 1:57 PM. We hadn't even left the house yet. Jenny had already gone to the church to help with the Children's program, so it was up to me as a dad to get Ryan there on time and in a presentable fashion. It was a real test of my paternal abilities.

Ryan, at the time, was a toddler and was to sing with the toddler group a song he didn't know and to be honest, none of the children probably knew. At that age, it is not about the kids' talent in singing, but the fact they are on stage and everyone can "ooh and aah" over how cute they are.

It was a simple act. A recording of C-H-R-I-S-T-M-A-S was to be played, and each child would "sing-along" while holding up the appropriate letter at the prompting of the teacher.

It was neither a German opera nor a Shakespearean act—it was just a trivial kid's program. After all, you can practice a hundred times with a group of toddlers, and it will be different 101 times. So why even practice? Just fly by the seat of your pants.

Most important, why do these children's workers need to interrupt my Saturday afternoon for this inconsequential rehearsal just as the Southeastern Conference Championship Football game comes on?

Fortunately, our parsonage was just one hundred yards from the church (the length of a football field), so I decided it would be quicker to walk. After all, it takes ten minutes just to get the car seat in order.

Ryan has always been a gregarious, happy child, but very self-determined. On that day, he *insisted* he wanted to walk and not be carried. That was not my plan. I could carry him and be there in no time, but with his toddler's feet, it would take forever. However, I yielded.

We began walking together, with Ryan holding my hand. It felt like I was in a slow-motion scene from the Six Million Dollar Man.

One of my many flaws is that I am a fast walker. Most people cannot keep up with me in just the average course of the day. I perfected the "walk and talk" so that I can kill two birds with one stone in a timely way. However, Ryan did not subscribe to my walking philosophy (and still does not to this day).

A patient dad would have stopped long enough to enjoy the moment, but that was not me. I let Ryan straggle along through about thirty steps and then my exasperation began. When he stumbled on the uneven path, I had all I could take, so I pulled him up brusquely to my side, announcing abruptly, "Ryan, we don't have time for this. Let's get a move on."

I honestly do not remember what Ryan did. He may have cried because I would not let him walk or he may have just compliantly enjoyed the unexpected ride on my hip. But what I do remember is a divine whisper in my ear that changed my perspective as a dad.

As soon as Ryan was on my hip and we were on the move, God whispered into my heart, "Aren't you glad I am not a father like you?"

In that surreal moment, it was just God and me, with Ryan along for the ride. God reminded me of many times I dragged my feet, or my stride did not match His sovereignty, but He patiently delayed for me as a loving father should pause for his child.

> *And the LORD passed by before him, and proclaimed, The LORD, The LORD God, merciful and gracious, longsuffering, and abundant in goodness and truth. – Exodus 34:6*

That which God softly spoke to me on that day along Carole Drive, He loudly and powerfully proclaimed from Mount Sinai as a sacred epilogue to the Ten Commandments. God did not merely say it, but He promised His mercy, grace, and longsuffering as a covenant by His passing before Moses. Exodus 34:6 is the first time in the Scripture the word "longsuffering" is used. It is used ten times in connection with God, four times in connection with man (Proverbs 14:29; 15:18; 16:32; Ecclesiastes 17:8), and once in connection with the wingspan of an eagle full of feathers. (Ezekiel 17:3).[iv]

It is easy to read my face when I am angry, but God's face does not display His anger toward His children when they are disobedient. Interestingly, according to Waltke when the Bible says God is "longsuffering" (Exodus 34:6; Numbers 14:18; Psalms 86:15, etc.), it literally reads, "God is long of nose."ᵛ When He is angry, His nose becomes inflamed and burns, but it does not quickly reach His face.

The face of God is essential in understanding the longsuffering of God.

For a moment, let's explore the context of the story. In Exodus 32, the children of Israel committed the sin of idolatry by building the golden calf. Idolatry is anything that replaces God in our lives, and God's children replaced Him with a creation of their own hands. What would God do to Israel?

In Exodus 33, the four-fold verdict is returned. First, God declared to Moses that Israel would see the fulfillment of His promise:

> *And the LORD said unto Moses, Depart, and go up hence, thou and the people which thou hast brought up out of the land of Egypt, unto the land which I sware unto Abraham, to Isaac, and to Jacob, saying, Unto thy seed will I give it.*
> *– Exodus 33:1*

God said Israel would rest in His protection:

> *And I will send an angel before thee;*
> *and I will drive out the Canaanite, the*
> *Amorite, and the Hittite, and the*
> *Perizzite, the Hivite, and the Jebusite.*
> *— Exodus 33:2*

God reminded Israel they would enjoy His provision:

> *Unto a land flowing with milk and*
> *honey. — Exodus 33:3a*

But Israel would lack His presence:

> *For I will not go up in the midst of*
> *thee; for thou art a stiffnecked people:*
> *lest I consume thee in the way. —*
> *Exodus 33:3*

God was prepared to no longer be an active Father, but turn over the care of His children to guardians and keepers. But just as any normal child doesn't like the extended absence of a parent; it was a frightening proposition for Moses. Therefore, Moses refused God's protection and provision unless God went with them into the Promised Land.

> *And he said unto him, If thy presence*
> *go not with me, carry us not up hence.*
> *– Exodus 33:15*

Just as any parent wearied with raising his children, God was tired of the wickedness of Israel. Thankfully, God is "long of nose" or longsuffering. In spite of the gross iniquity of Israel, His nose was burning, but it never reached His face.

God relented and showed grace unto Moses on behalf of Israel, and at which, Moses made an unusual request:

> *And he said, I beseech thee, shew me*
> *thy glory. – Exodus 33:19*

Now notice this. God graciously responded that He would make all His "goodness" pass before Moses as he hid in the cleft of the rock. However, if Moses were to look upon the face of God, Moses would not live. So God's glory (His countenance) would pass by, and Moses would be covered by God's hand. God would then remove His hand to display His hinder parts (His goodness).

In other words, God's goodness is the filtered form of God's glory.

The next day, God passed before Moses and God revealed his goodness while announcing His grace, mercy, and patience. God is more concerned with His declaration than in offering an explanation. That is what makes God's goodness so great, and Moses recognized it, and immediately Moses fell to his face and worshipped God.

Allow me to stop here to say that if you are waiting to see the glory of God to worship Him, then you are wrong. If you cannot worship God in response to His goodness, why do you think He will reveal His glory to you? Many Christians focus on knowing God in some otherworldly experience rather than enjoying intimacy with God in His goodness. And primary in His goodness is His mercy, grace, and longsuffering.

There are those sacred moments when God passes before us to remind us of His goodness. The Hebrew word in Exodus 34:6 for passed *by before* is the same word employed in Exodus 12:12 and 23 speaking of the night of the "pass over." God promised not only to *pass through* the land of Egypt and smite the disobedient but *pass over* the obedient.

God's passing before Moses revealed the dividing line of God's goodness—a clear boundary between mercy and judgment, grace and vengeance, and longsuffering and wrath. God made a covenant of patience with His children—the children of Israel.

If there has ever been a group of children that would try the patience of the most benevolent father, it would be this bunch.

They whined and wailed, threw temper tantrums, and were incorrigibly sassy, continually complaining about their dinner. And on a forty-year road trip through the wilderness, these children relentlessly moaned, "Are we there yet? Are we there yet?" As impatient as the children of Israel were, their Father was even more patient.

After all, He promised to be.

God knew His children, in their fallen nature, would break His commands. His demand was not for perfection, but for obedience. Perfection is not within reach of any of His children, but obedience is. So He promised He would not be a "one-strike-and-you-are-out" kind of dad. He is longsuffering.

You see, we all have experienced God's mercy and grace. But it was not a one-time event. Every day we need to ask forgiveness for sins we have committed, and God in His longsuffering is willing to give His grace and mercy again and again.

So why can't I show longsuffering toward my toddling son's stumble? Why can't Christians give grace toward those overtaken in a fault (Galatians 6:1)? Why can't you forgive that person who offended you?

The ancient rabbis tell a story of Abraham inviting into his tent a man who, at suppertime, offered no thanks to God for His mercy. Frustrated by the man's ingratitude and disregard, the patriarch threw him out of his tent into the desert hungry and homeless.

Later in the night, God woke Abraham, saying to him, "Where is the guest?"

Abraham said, "When he did not fear You or offer You thanks, I sent him away."

God reprimanded Abraham, saying, "Who made you his judge? I have borne with him all these years. Could you not bear with him one night? Have you learned nothing from my mercy to you?"[vi]

In truth, we are a product of God's good patience and forbearance. When we pause to remember the longsuffering mercy we have received, it is then that we should be more willing to grant it to others.

Two Christians were driving through an area where the road was being widened. At the end of the repair zone, a sign informed travelers, "Construction Ended. Thank You for Your Patience."

"I think that would make an appropriate gravestone epitaph for my life," said one of the Christians.

I think it would be for all of us. None of us have arrived. Some of us have not even departed. If God can be patient with us, surely we can display the fruit of the Spirit of longsuffering toward others.

There have been plenty of times as I was walking with God, holding His hand when I suddenly stumbled. I am grateful He did not jolt me up as I did Ryan, but He was full of mercy, grace, and patience.

So back to the question, God whispered in my heart, "Aren't you glad I am not a father like you?" The answer is a resounding "YES!"

> *It is of the LORD'S mercies that we are not consumed, because his compassions fail not. They are new every morning: great is thy faithfulness.*
> *– Lamentations 3:22, 23*

# CHAPTER FOUR

# Make Them Stop, Daddy!

It was early one morning in 2002 when I had to take Ryan to the hospital for a blood draw. Ryan, just under age two, already had white coat anxiety from previous visits and shots in the past. But he was about to go through something he had never experienced before.

The phlebotomist came in with six large vials to be used to collect his blood. I wondered if he would have any blood left when she was done.

She was a sweet lady who had a hard job to do. As best she could, she tried to keep the moment relaxed and comfortable. So she said, "Dad, why don't you sit in this chair, and you let Ryan climb up into your lap?"

She instructed me to hug him tight, and one technician would try to distract him while the other would hold his little arm to insert the catheter to draw the blood.

The distraction didn't work.

Tears welled up in my little man's eyes, and I heard four words from Ryan that left me feeling so helpless. "Make them stop, Daddy."

I hugged him closer and couldn't say a word. I once again was an emotional mess. It had to be done; his blood had to be drawn.

Over and over again, Ryan cried, "Make them stop, Daddy! Daddy! Please make them stop!"

Each time I heard those words, my heart was broken.

When our church family commemorates communion, I remember that moment with Ryan and wonder if perhaps that was what the Father felt when the Son was on the Cross and the nails were driven into His hands and feet.

"Make them stop, Daddy!" was not heard. But instead, Jesus said, "Father, forgive them for they know what they do" (Luke 23:34).

The phlebotomist taking my son's blood was a sweet older lady, but I was getting angry with her as time went along and as I heard my son's cries. I can only imagine the Father's wrath seething as He watched His only begotten Son writhing in pain as a world that did not understand or appreciate His sacrifice mocked and jeered at His Son.

By no means do I minimize the pain of the Cross as being equal to a blood draw from a little boy. But I do say, I felt for a brief moment a small portion of the grief the Father felt as He watched His Son dying for six hours on the Cross. May we never forget the sorrow of the Father as He watched Him die in agony and blood.

When I hold that cup of juice that symbolizes the shed blood of the Son of God, I hear my little boy saying, "Make them stop, Daddy!"

*There is a fountain filled with blood*
*Drawn from Immanuel's veins;*
*And sinners, plunged beneath that flood,*
*Lose all their guilty stains:*
*Lose all their guilty stains,*
*Lose all their guilty stains;*
*And sinners, plunged beneath that flood,*
*Lose all their guilty stains.*

# CHAPTER FIVE
## *Exceeding, Abundantly*

Each of us has struggles that we are facing, have faced, or will face that will add definition to the portrait of our lives. For my wife and me, something like this happened about fifteen years ago as of this writing. We had struggled with infertility for a few years, and after much prayer, we experienced God's wonderful provision through adoption. Looking back, we can say we saw the provision of the Lord when He gave us a son that belonged in our home and will always be in our hearts.

We had anticipated that, after Ryan's adoption, we would never have any more children for three reasons. First, we did not think we could withstand the emotional journey again. Secondly, our adoption agency would not permit a second placement so that other waiting couples could have an opportunity to adopt. Finally, our financial resources had been tapped out, and we could not pursue another adoption through a different agency.

That first year with Ryan was heaven on earth. The first seven years of our marriage had been filled with an empty cradle and a silent house, but now it was filled with the laughter and the cries of a baby.

But that was not enough for us. The more we enjoyed and loved Ryan, the more God gave us a desire to have more children. Some accused us of being selfish in wanting more children. A few said we should be happy with the one miracle God had given us, "and don't go back to the well a second time." However, Jenny and I both knew God was working in our lives.

Finally, when we came to terms with the fact that we both had a God-given desire for more children, but the possibility of having more seemed to be beyond our reach, we began to pray about it. We became very transparent about our desire for more children, and we invited some extraordinary and godly people into our home to pray with us about seeking God's timing and provision for this desire. These prayer warriors prayed with us and encouraged us as real friends.

I have always believed that where God guides, He provides. I knew that if God had guided us to this honorable desire, He would provide. We were willing to pursue any opportunity that God would open. We looked at other adoption agencies but found no peace from the Lord. I knew that I could get the financial resources for another adoption, but would that be the route God took to complete our family miraculously? Looking back now, I know God was closing doors on possibilities that I could have manipulated to make work on my own. I would have missed the true miracle He wanted for us if I had.

After much prayer, we returned to our doctor and expressed our desire to have more children. Our doctor referred us to an infertility specialist, and before we knew it, we were on the dark journey we had hoped to avoid. My take charge, type-A personality was up for the challenge, and I would coach and cajole my wife through the process, believing it was God's will.

After extensive testing, the specialists determined that there was no physical reason we should not be able to have "a quiver full" of children, but diagnosed us with unexplained infertility.

That is the worst of diagnoses—that of "unexplained." If the doctor would have said, "There is a medical abnormality, and it is impossible for you to have children," we could have accepted it. "Impossibility" meant we should move on to adoption again. "Unexplained" left us in fertility limbo.

Now it became a painful, personal struggle.

Laura Bush, the wife of President George W. Bush, poignantly wrote about her struggle with infertility in her book *Spoken from the Heart:*

> The English language lacks the words to mourn an absence. For the loss of a parent, grandparent, spouse, child or friend, we have all manner of words and phrases, some helpful some not. Still we are conditioned to say something, even if it is only "I'm sorry for your loss." But for an absence, for someone who was never there at all, we are wordless to capture that particular emptiness. For those who deeply want children and are denied them, those missing babies hover like silent ephemeral shadows over their lives. Who can describe the feel of a tiny hand that is never held?[vii]

Our hope had turned to frustrated grief. Our partially empty arms had become a heavy burden we could not bear. God had given us a desire, but no means to see it fulfilled—apart from His working. We began a year and a half journey of fertility drugs and evaluations. The emotional lows and losses were tremendous. Seeing my wife grieve as she did and the unbearable sense of helplessness I felt for her sent me into a dark depression. Unfortunately, my faith weakened to the point where I was ready to give up the ministry. I suppose I thought I would "get back" at God for the cruel trick He had played on Jenny and me.

Jenny and I finally just gave up. Confused and frustrated, we told God, "We are content with the one miracle You have given us in Ryan. And while we don't understand the desire You placed in our hearts for more children, we accept that You are not going to do it, and so we give up."

An unusual, unexplainable peace came over my wife. I wish I could say that peace came to me. However, her faith that everything would be okay was so strong, that she strengthened my faith. Jenny just gave it all over to the Lord, and the Lord strengthened her heart with a verse:

> *"For the vision is yet for an appointed time, but at the end it shall speak, and*

> *not lie: though it tarry, wait for it;*
> *because it will surely come, it will not*
> *tarry."*
> *– Habakkuk 2:3*

Jenny's faith was strong enough to believe that God was going to do what was sovereignly right for our family, and we just needed to "let go and let God" work in His time. Someone once told me that great faith is not seen in getting what you want from God, but great faith is seen in accepting what God gives as best. After the emotional distress of a year and a half, we finally were there.

Abraham and Sarah were there. For seventy years they had been childless, and they reached the point of acceptance. But one day, a holy Visitor comes with an announcement that they would have a child.

Sarah was eavesdropping behind the tent door, and when she heard the announcement, she burst out with laughter. Not for joy, but with skepticism, because the long delay of God in fulfilling the promise seemed to contradict nature's denial. In Genesis 17:17, when the Lord reiterated the promise to Abraham that they were going to have a son, Abraham fell upon his face and laughed out of joyful faith. Sarah laughed, but it was the laugh of disbelief. She laughed aloud, but questioned in her heart, "How can I bear a child in old age?"

Then the holy Visitor queried, "Is anything too hard for the Lord?"

The Hebrew term for "too hard" is applied to man around fifteen times in Scripture. In those instances, the original word means "to be beyond one's capabilities," and therefore impossible or inaccessible. And such are God's mighty and incomprehensible acts.

Two verses in Jeremiah (32:17, 27) are almost identical to this rhetorical question asked in Genesis 18:14. The understood answer is a resounding NO!

That question is *never* asked in the New Testament. What the Old Testament questioned, the New Testament answered.

Let's visit a little home in Nazareth. We find a young teenage girl named Mary who has just been told two astounding facts by another holy visitor. First, she was told that she would be the mother of the Son of God by divine conception. That announcement was shocking in and of itself. But as a confirmation of God's ability, the birth announcement was made that her Aunt Elizabeth, who is geriatric in age, was pregnant with her husband Zacharias' son.

Then the visitor concludes with this declaration, "For with God nothing shall be impossible."

Outside a Bedouin tent in the plains of the Negev desert, the question was asked, "Is anything too hard for the Lord?"

For centuries that question echoed through the lives of Rebekah, Hannah, Manoah, and countless others, but it is not until Mary that the question was answered: "For with God nothing shall be impossible."

Anything hard in our lives becomes possible with God. The depth of our problem does not limit the strength of His power.

A. W. Pink places this reality in perspective when he wrote, "How can we who are so weak in ourselves, so inferior in power to the enemies confronting us, bear up under our trials which are so numerous, so protracted, so crushing? We could not, and therefore Divine grace has provided for us an all-sufficient Helper. Without His aid, we had long since succumbed, mastered by our trials. Hope looks forward to the Glory to come; in the weary interval of waiting, the Spirit supports our poor hearts and keeps grace alive within us."[viii]

Paul Harvey used to say, "And now the rest of the story."

Three months later, after coming to a place of relative peace about not having any other children, Jenny breaks the news to me that she has not been feeling well and her flu-like symptoms would not go away. I knew something was going on when, at our favorite restaurant, she pushed a plate of her favorite food away and said, "That doesn't taste right." Then she started getting weepy, not crying out of sorrow, but just emotional over the silliest things. A commercial on television could begin the river of tears. It was only then that I realized she wasn't depressed, but that her hormones were raging!

With disbelieving hope, we contacted the doctors, and they confirmed it—she was pregnant—with not one, but two healthy babies. Those two healthy babies have grown into two beautiful daughters we named Jenna and Maggie.

They are my monuments to God who works miracles when we can't. When I face a struggle that seems insurmountable, I look at my daughters who remind me to "stand still and see the salvation of the Lord."

God was not only gracious, but mighty in that, He didn't give us one additional child as we asked Him, but twins! God did exceedingly and abundantly above what we asked.

Two years later, God did exceedingly and abundantly above what we thought. Yes, two years later, Jenny found out she was expecting our son, Josiah. We had never imagined having a family of four children. We had been just praying for one more—a sibling for our Ryan.

Out of the darkest and potentially most devastating struggle of our married life and my adult life, God strengthened our marriage and faith. But it wasn't until we gave up and gave in to God's undisclosed will that we experienced the greatest blessing of life.

Now I have four monuments to God's miraculous ability in spite of our incapability. When my daughters climb into my lap after a long day to say, "I love you, Daddy," it is God reminding me to rest in His everlasting love through the battles I face. When my two competitive sons (whom I have nicknamed the sons of thunder) want to pass the football or play basketball in the driveway, it is God's way of showing me that when the battle seems impossible, it is not won in my strength or ability, but by His sufficient grace. When we sit together around the dinner table, and I am frustrated by the noise and the mess, I quietly pause in the chaos to be still for a moment and thank God there is not anything that is too hard for Him.

CHAPTER SIX

# *Rumors and Stories of War*

As best as we could, we wanted our children always to get along and never express anger or wrath toward one another. However, that ideal was never met.

If you need the reason, skip ahead and read the next chapter on our children's strong will. The purpose of this chapter is to show the difference between fighting *with* your sibling and fighting *for* your sibling.

Let's face it, as parents; we cannot stop our kids from getting bumps and bruises from bullies in life. Sometimes our kids are the bullies.

A perfect example of familial bullies was several years back. It was a weekend when my wife's sister and husband came to visit and brought their two children.

Cousins!

That always makes a weekend fun. When cousins come, the kids seem to divide up into gender-based clans and engage in impressive feats of strength. It was boys versus girls all weekend.

I wasn't there that afternoon of the shot that was heard around the world—or at least around the neighborhood. But I have listened to the story enough from all four of my kids that I feel I can tell it in the first person.

The kids were playing whiffle ball in the backyard. In addition to being strong-willed, my kids are competitive. It wasn't long before I heard a kerfuffle brewing in the yard.

Ryan's voice rose, "Jenna, it was out!"

"No, it wasn't. It was in, and you just missed it," Jenna responded with staccato, machine-gun like cadence.

"The only way you can win is by cheating. You don't get that point," Ryan declared like an Olympic judge who had just discovered performance-enhancing drugs in a locker room.

Slowly, the crescendo of excited voices rose as the discourse quickly lowered.

Jenna said, "If you don't shut up, I am going to throw this (holding up a whiffle racket) at you."

"No, you won't because you aren't brave enough to do it, and even if you did, you would miss," Ryan retorted smugly. But then he pulled the trigger. He said the nickname his sisters abhorred.

You see this was the name Ryan has always called his sisters to get under their skin. In fact, to this day, he still says it, and it drives me crazy too.

"Sussy."

Parenthetically, I don't know where he got that name. I honestly think, when he was little, he was trying to say "sissy," and it came out "sussy" and stuck.

Ryan is notorious for making new words out of original ones. Zebego for "gazebo" and sacardager for "massager" are two that comes to mind immediately, and we don't let him forget.

But on that particular day, "Sussy" was the final straw. It was like Japan's attack on Pearl Harbor or the planes crashing into the Twin Towers. A disproportional response was warranted.

As soon as Ryan said "Sussy" the story instantly transformed into a slow-motion scene from an overly dramatic movie.

Jenna stiffened, standing like little David with sling and stone in hand. Then she raised the whiffle racquet like a sword in the grip of General

Gideon and swung her arm around a couple of times only to release the racquet from her hand with precision accuracy.

In seeming slow motion, the whiffle racquet moved across the backyard making a whistling, whizzing sound simultaneously. A sound much like a Herlitzer bomb hurling from the sky.

Witz…witz…witz…witz…witz…THUD.

Impact.

The whiffle racquet landed squarely across the bridge of Ryan's nose.

Ryan was stunned, and Jenna's siblings and cousins were silent.

"I told you I would do it – and I did!" Jenna announced.

To this day, Ryan's nose bears a scar, or better put, the imprint of a rounded edge of a whiffle racquet. And on that day, he gained a new respect for his sister.

Now before you think Jenny and I endorsed or encouraged this behavior, you are wrong. There is nothing that grieves me more as a parent than to hear of my children fighting.

But looking back on it, we all laugh about it now. Sometimes when Ryan gets out of hand, Jenna threatens to get her whiffle racquet.

I share all of that to say: siblings fight. But the whole battle could have been averted if Jenna had just come and told me what Ryan had done or was saying. I would have stepped in and stopped matters from escalating to the point where plastic surgery or facial reconstruction might have been needed.

In complete transparency, extreme fights like that don't often happen in our home. Our kids squabble often, but occasionally those squabbles become fights that are knock-down, dragged out brawls. And it should not be that way. Just as it should not be this way in our earthly homes, it should not be so in our eternal family because we are the children of our Heavenly Father with a new nature.

But brotherly battle-royals even happened in early church times. James wrote:

> *From whence come wars and fightings*
> *among you? come they not hence, even*
> *of your lusts that war in your*
> *members?*
> *– James 4:1*

Quarrels and fights were part of the early church family and still are to this day. But just because they are present doesn't mean it is right.

It's interesting the words that are used in James 4:1. The word "fight" is the Greek word *machomai*. It means hand to hand combat. It was a word that was used in the classical Greek to describe the Spartans.

The Spartans were some of the most vicious, cruel soldiers of Greek history. They weren't like the Athenians military who were more of an aristocratic soldier. No, the Spartans would be more like the Navy SEALS—only they were trained from childhood for this task. Boys who trained in Sparta would often be sent alone into the wilderness for weeks at a time to toughen them up. They encouraged viciousness and callousness. Their food was rarely pleasant, but full of grit and filth to get them used to combat conditions. They were taught to kill, brutally in any way or means necessary.

James then used the word "war" to describe this sibling rivalry. Interestingly, it is used seven times in the New Testament. One time is found in James, another in 1 Corinthians, and five others in Revelation. The five references in Revelation all deal with spiritual conflict such as when Satan goes to war with God.

May I be bold to declare that when we accuse and fight with our brothers and sisters in Christ, we are displaying a demonic and diabolical attitude. When we would rather fight and war than pray and ask our Heavenly Father to mend the relationship, we are behaving just like Satan.

As uncomfortable as that sounds, we are all born with this desire. Just look at any child. Who taught them to demand, to take without asking, to argue over which toy belongs to whom, or to react maliciously when they don't get their way? No one did. We are all born like that and need to have this attitude trained out of us. As adults, we have merely refined this attitude, but it makes it no less demonic.

The words "fights" and "wars" is what James used to describe the conflicts that occur among *you*—the family of God. And interestingly, the context of James question is our prayer life. Essentially, James is saying, "How can you pray to your Father when you are fighting with your Father's child (your brother or sister)?"

How it must grieve our Father when He sees us fighting with our spiritual siblings!

It would be wise here, however, to give one final story of when it is right to fight.

Years ago, all four of our kids were outside playing, and a new kid, not from our neighborhood, joined the gang. He was a loudmouth kind of kid about the same age as Josiah.

Again, this is second-hand information, told from all three of my kids who were eyewitnesses. Therefore, I share a synoptic gospel of those events that day.

This mouthy kid began to say some very inappropriate, unkind things to and about Ryan. Ryan, who was older and stronger, decided not to retaliate, so he walked away.

Let me stop there and say how proud I was of Ryan at that moment. As the old preacher used to say, "A dog can whip a skunk, but it's just not worth it." He could have allowed his anger to get the best of him, but he thought better of it and realized it wasn't worth it.

However, as Ryan was walking away, the kid got louder and continued to say some very hurtful things.

Then he suddenly stopped talking.

Josiah had picked him up and dropped him on the ground. Ryan turned around to see his brother standing over this punk with his finger in his face, saying, "You don't say that about my brother or you have to deal with me."

Again, Jenny and I do not endorse or encourage this behavior, but I have to say that when I heard the story, I thought, "YESSS!!! They get it!"

Ryan walked away as he should have. But Josiah stood up for his brother.

Proverbs 17:17 says:

*A friend loveth at all times, and a brother is born for adversity.*

You see, Jenny and I want to train our children that we stick together as a family. We don't fight *with* each other, but we should be willing to fight *for* one another.

I have a feeling our Heavenly Father feels the same way.

# CHAPTER SEVEN

# The Gift of a Strong Will

Stubborn.

That's the one word I could use to describe myself. But when I describe my wife, who has the same quality, I would never use the same word. Instead, I say "strong-willed." It sounds a little politer that way.

Yes, it is possible for a stubborn husband and a strong-willed wife to have a blessed marriage. We've made our marriage work because our marriage has been and is a work in progress. Ephesians 5:21 has taught us to be submissive to each other when appropriate and meekly stand our ground and speak our minds when necessary. Honestly, one of the most attractive qualities I found in Jenny (and there are many) was her strong will. Someone wisely said, "Don't marry the person you think you can live with; marry only the individual you think you can't live without," and I did just that.

To conceive children that have homogenized our personalities could be dangerous. The lab workers at the Oak Ridge National Laboratory who unknowingly worked on the Atom Bomb did not have the amount of destructive force available to them as they could have had in the blending of the stubborn and strong-willed personalities of Jon and Jenny Lands.

The Lands household has four nuclear warheads in its familial arsenal. Yes, I said four. All four children have an extra dose of strong wills, which lends itself the question: is a strong will an inherited or learned trait?

I say both. It is both nature and nurture that develops this trait.

Ryan's first bout of stubbornness came while Jenny and I were still young, naïve parents. Jenny had read all the books on Christian parenting and could give me a ready answer for a crisis *before* it happened. But *when* it arrived, she would melt down. I, on the other hand, just knew everything from the general observation of the parenting failures of others (written tongue in cheek). After that first test of wills between Ryan and his "perfect" parents, all theories were thrown out the door.

We had to take three other remedial courses on this matter of stubbornness because each one of our children progressively increased by birth order in obstinacy.

I remember a lady once offered to purchase me a copy of James Dobson's *The Strong-Willed Child* after encountering Josiah's obstinacy. I told her "Ma'am, I have read it. In fact, James Dobson is doing a case study on our children."

In all seriousness, *The Strong-Willed Child* is an excellent and helpful book. Dr. Dobson reminds us in the book, "The Lord gave me this challenging child for a purpose. He wants me to mold and shape this youngster and prepare him or her for a life of service to Him."[ix]

Did you catch that? Mold. Shape. That's what we are to do with our strong-willed child.

With that, I am going to say something that may ruffle some feathers. I am thankful for my children's strong will. I wasn't grateful for it when we clashed in the terrible twos, and I still get wearied dealing with it in the testy teen years. But I am thankful for the strong will in my children.

I remember reading magazines on the great joy of parenting that would almost gleefully write about the harsh punishment necessary to *break* the will of a child. It was a parenting style of all justice and no grace. And even then, I knew the parent's job is not to *break* the child's will but to *bend* it.

Shape. Mold. Bend.

You see, you cannot say you believe in the doctrine of the free will of man in relationship to our Heavenly Father when you attempt to eradicate the strong free will in your child.

The most common definition of free will is the ability to make choices without any prior prejudice, inclination, or disposition. In *The Freedom of the Will*, Jonathan Edwards defines biblical freedom as a man being free to choose according to his disposition.[x] Humans always decide according to their strongest desire, and thus we make free choices. To put it bluntly, humanly speaking, we do what we want to do.

Taking this into consideration, would you agree that the highest rebellion is that of a man who rejects God? I would. But God doesn't override or overrule any man or woman's rebellious will. Our Father gently entreats and calls them to come to Him, as the old Puritan writers said, "God woos the unbeliever." Even when a believer, His child, sins, our Heavenly Father doesn't pounce on the wayward child with divine judgment the first time they stumble. No, He graciously speaks to their heart a word of conviction. If His child digs his heels in and continues his disobedient path, there is a definite escalation of chastisement (Hebrews 12:5-11).

The same is true in parenting a strong-willed child. We don't just pour out on a child massive judgment when that stubborn free will chooses to sin. Through a process of grace-filled correction, we guide the child to a place of rightness. The child must be corrected, but if he continues in that same rebellious choice, then we escalate from correction to chastisement. If we follow the example of our Heavenly Father, we won't skip correction and jump immediately to chastisement.

I once heard a wise parent say, "An accusation hardens the will, but a question stirs the conscience." Have you ever noticed that our Heavenly Father corrects us with questions and not with harsh accusations?

When Adam chose to sin in his own free will, God comes to the Garden and asks the question, "Adam, where are you?" (Genesis 3:9). Now God knew where Adam was, after all, He is omniscient and omnipresent. But by asking the question, He wanted Adam to recognize it and respond. God didn't come down off the front porch of heaven grabbing a switch ready to pounce on Adam and Eve in punitive anger, but He wanted to speak to the heart of their free will. Yes, there was correction and chastisement, but He spoke first to the heart of man. That is how we shape, mold, and bend that strong freewill in our children.

A strong freewill in a child or adult is not a bad thing, so long as it is bent in the right direction. I think it has been possible that in our well-intentioned desire to "break the will" of our children as parents we have crossed the thin line that results in their broken spirit.

In fact, as parents of toddler's we often mistake God's gift of free will as something sinful. Whether in a child or adult, there is a difference in being *rebellious* and being *resolute*. A parent would do well to recognize the difference and act accordingly. Mistaking resolution as rebellion could easily break the spirit of the child.

James Dobson writes, "Harshness, gruffness, and sternness are not effective in shaping a child's will. Likewise, constant whacking and threatening and criticizing are destructive and counterproductive. A parent who is mean and angry most of the time is creating resentment that will be stored and come roaring into the relationship during adolescence or beyond. Therefore, every opportunity should be taken to keep the tenor of the home pleasant, fun, and accepting. At the same time, however, parents should display certain firmness in their demeanor.

You, Mom and Dad, are the boss. You are in charge. If you believe it, the tougher child will accept it also."[xi]

Don't misunderstand Dobson's premise. He is not saying parents should let their children run wild. He is saying that parenting a strong-willed child doesn't require *anger* but *action*.

Isn't that how God our Father responds to our rebellious will?

> *The LORD is merciful and gracious, slow to anger, and plenteous in mercy.*
> *– Psalm 103:8*

> *The LORD is gracious, and full of compassion; slow to anger, and of great mercy.*
> *– Psalm 145:8*

Some people view God as a father who looks down from heaven with a sovereign scowl on his face and a white-knuckled grip on a celestial mallet ready to destroy us when we do wrong.

No. Our Father is gracious, merciful, and slow to anger.

With that gracious mercy, God trains and teaches us the way we should go so that every moment is a life lesson from which we can learn.

*For the grace of God...Teaching us*
*that, denying ungodliness and worldly*
*lusts, we should live soberly, righteously,*
*and godly, in this present world.*
*– Titus 2:11-12*

God doesn't take away our free will, but He does seek to make sure our choices are right by the influence of His grace.

And as a child grows, so will his expression of free will. For what it's worth, child psychologists tell us children fully develop their understanding of the free will between ages four and five. I don't know if I fully accept that as a psychological truth, but I do find it interesting that most children raised in a Christian home begin to understand at that young age their sinfulness and their need for a Savior.

I came to Christ at the age of five, and I know for sure that I did so of my own free will. I placed my full faith and trust in Christ's work on the Cross for my sin. My children came to Christ around that age as well. These strong-willed gifts from God accepted the greatest gift of God by choosing to know and follow Him.

With that, please understand that the role of the parent is to progressively teach our children to make the right choices, not make the decisions for them. And that should be our goal in parenting; to bend or shape the free will of our sometimes stubborn child in the proper direction so they can demonstrate the qualities of Bible characters of strong will. Why? Because a child needs a strong will to live the distinct Christian life in a post-Christian era.

Moses had to have a strong will to outlast the stubbornness of the Pharaoh and demand, "Let my people go!"

Shadrach, Meshach, and Abednego knew the king's demand was idolatrous and they did not waver in standing up for God. They trusted He would secure them and give them the grace to withstand the weight of the King's pressure. In the end, God received the glory and Shadrach, Meshach, and Abednego was protected. Had the three Hebrew children not had that strong-will and trust in the Lord, they would have easily bent to the desires of others.

We too will experience that crushing pressure to follow the crowd. However, when we are confronted with nothing but hard choices, we still must stand up for what we believe. But at that moment God reinforces our strong-will with a strength and grace to take that stand.

What about Esther? Even though she was the wife of the King, he didn't know she was Jewish.

King Ahasuerus had been persuaded to dispose of all Jews, and at first, Esther was fearful of making a move. At that point, her cousin, Mordecai, reminded Esther that she was given her royal opportunity "for such a time as this." Mordecai advised her that God would give her the wisdom and fortitude to use her position to protect their people.

Esther is the reminder that we are where we are for a purpose, and God has given us our opportunity so we can make a difference. But Esther couldn't have made a difference if she had not doggedly gone before King Ahasuerus to reveal Haman's plot.

That's just a few examples from Scripture. The same determination and strong-will required in Moses, the three Hebrew children, and Esther are needed in spades to stand up for Christ today. It is my God-given role as a parent to follow God's model as our Heavenly Father to bend the free will of my children.

So, looking back, when Ryan pitched a fit about eating his vegetables and refused to eat, that was the beginning of a backbone in Ryan that, while wrong in attitude, was similar to the spine fully and properly displayed in Daniel's refusing to eat the king's meat. When Maggie refused to go to bed as a toddler and climbed out of her baby bed and marched defiantly into the living room to "be with Daddy," a kernel of the spirit Esther was revealed. When Josiah tackled a neighbor kid and, as we say down south, "put a whoopin' on 'em" for poking fun at his sibling, a grain of Moses sprouted up!

I'm not making excuses for bad behavior, but I am offering hope for a better character. Looking back, I wish I had responded as graciously as my Heavenly Father had and attempted to shape their strong will rather than overrule it.

May we never forget that the free will to make right choices requires a strong will to continue in those choices.

# CHAPTER EIGHT

# A Garden or Greenhouse?

There is nothing better for supper at the end of a hot summer day than a tomato sandwich (at least for me). Two pieces of white bread, slathered with mayonnaise, and a thick slice of a garden grown tomato.

Mmm...Mmm....good. It is so good that I think tomato sandwiches will be on the menu for the Marriage Supper of the Lamb in heaven.

But there is one descriptive word that makes the sandwich so heavenly.

Garden.

Yes, garden grown tomatoes are the beefiest and tastiest. Now I've had those weak tomatoes you can buy at the supermarket, and they don't compare in size or succulence.

Do you know what makes the difference? The environment in which the tomato is grown. The perfect climate of a greenhouse with constant temperature and consistent light along with a perfectly timed watering can make reasonably uniform tomatoes.

But they are not tasty.

The reason a garden grown tomato is so tasty is that it wasn't sheltered in a perfect environment. The garden grown tomato experienced some hard storms and splatters of mud and manure, along with the droughts when they were near death. But the difficulty of the environment made the tomato better and beefier.

You say, Jon, what in the world does this have to do with raising children and our Heavenly Father?

I'm glad you asked. *Everything.*

As a pastor, I have noticed two basic styles of Christian parenting: garden grown children and greenhouse children.

The greenhouse child is raised in a seemingly perfect environment and wrapped in bubble wrap by the zealously over-prepared and often controlling parent. But the garden grown child is cared for by the gardener who recognizes that some storms and difficult circumstances build a strong character in the child. Yes, the gardener tends the garden, picking out the weeds and rocks, but doesn't control the weather, whether it floods or there is a drought.

Similarly, that's what our Heavenly Father does for us. He leaves us in the garden that He tends as the gardener.

Jesus put it this way in His high priestly prayer: "I pray not that thou shouldest take them out of the world, but that thou shouldest keep them from the evil" (John 17:15).

Our Father's plan is to leave us *in* the world (a garden), but in His care; He protects us *from* the Evil One as the gardener.

That is a model we are to follow as moms and dads. We are to allow the hard-knocks and difficulties of life to strengthen and shape the character of our children. It is the difference between *being* a parent and parenting.

An odd thing occurred to mothers and fathers and children at the close of the 20th century. It was called "parenting." From the beginning, mothers and fathers have taken special care of children. But the term "parenting" didn't appear in the United States until the late 1950s. According to the Merriam-Webster dictionary, the term "parenting" became common only in the 1970s. The term "parenting" has come to be favored over parenthood, child-rearing, and bringing up, particularly in sociological and educational literature and in popular writing.[xii]

Today "parenting" means something that parents should *do* not *be*. Today "to parent" is a goal-oriented action word; it describes a job with potential rewards. The basic aim of "parenting" is to stroke the adult's ego by making a child the best, happiest or most successful. Parenting plasters bumper stickers on the SUV announcing, "My child is an All-Star Student at Middle America Elementary."

Parenting quietly compares our children to everyone else's and smugly says my child is better because of my "parenting skills." It is the self-righteous attitude that believes the right kind of "parenting" will produce the right kind of child, who in turn will become the right kind of adult.

That's why multiplied millions of dollars have been made on books, videos, and seminars about better "parenting" techniques. There are 60,000 books in the parenting section on Amazon and even more in Christian bookstores, and many of them offering practical advice on "how to" raise your children.[xiii] And with each new idea that is packaged and propagated to new parents, there comes new controversy.

We debate over issues like when your baby cries at night, should you hold and comfort him or let him cry it out? Which is safest: strollers facing front or back? Should children have homework, and if so, how much homework? How much screen time on electronics should a child have, if at all?

Particularly in the Christian culture, we are so focused on the *responsibilities* of "parenting" that we don't understand our *role* as parents.

It is the difference between tomatoes raised in a greenhouse versus a garden. The former emphasizes the *procedure*, while the latter focuses on the *produce*.

We are not raising cookie-cutter children as every child is fearfully and wonderfully made (Psalm 139:14). As parents, we are instructed to "train up a child in the way *he* should go" (Proverbs 22:6). Not every child is bent in the same direction. I see that in my own home.

Ryan is an intelligent, articulate young man with a tendency toward analytical thinking; he enjoys listening to music but has no desire to learn an instrument. While Josiah is just as intelligent and articulate, he is more of a doer than a thinker. Josiah is athletic and musically inclined, and he loves to play the piano.

If we were following the greenhouse model, we would have tried to raise all four of our children in the same way. All our children must take piano. All our children must be athletic. All must be straight

A students. But that is just impossible because each child is unique. Each child has his or her own set of strengths and weaknesses. That means our role as parents is expressed differently based on the individuality of each child's personality.

Jesus said in the teaching on the vine and the branches in John 15 that the Father is the vinedresser. Note "the vinedresser" is a noun, not a verb. Let's remember that "parent" is not a verb, but a noun.

We must never forget that to be a parent is to be part of a weighty and unique God-given relationship, to engage in a particular kind of love.

Instead of valuing "parenting," we should treasure "being a parent." Instead of thinking about caring for children as a kind of work, aimed at producing smart, happy or successful adults, we should think of it as a kind of love. Love doesn't have objectives or targets or designs, but it does have a purpose. As a parent, love's mission is raising children of character while embracing their unique personalities and gifts.

Raising children is like tending a garden, and the role of a parent is like being a gardener. When we garden, we toil and sweat, and we're often covered in mud and manure. But we do it to create a protected and nurturing space for tender plants to grow and flourish.

# CHAPTER NINE
## *Keep Dead Dogs Buried!*

Two months after Jenny and I were married, we had our first baby, a fully grown black Labrador Retriever. In fact, for the first seven years of our marriage, this dog named Rondy was our baby.

She was named Rondy because she came into our lives while we lived in Alaska. She was named after the Anchorage sled-dog race, the *Fur Rendezvous*. And Rondy traveled with us from Alaska back to Tennessee, and finally to West Virginia.

Seven years later, our Ryan came along, and Rondy became his dog too. She was protective of him like a big sister should be. And he grew up with her as his dog.

But it seemed that, after Ryan was born, time sped up. Four years later, his sisters were born. And while our home was filled with the joy of young children, little did we realize our old dog was struggling.

By 2005, Rondy was losing control of her bowels and suffered from hip dysplasia which made it hard for her to navigate the stairs in our home.

I knew that things were not going to improve for our 15-year-old dog, and I didn't want to see her suffer. So I called the veterinarian to inquire as to what to do.

I hated that conversation. It was uncomfortable. How much did it cost? How do they do it? What to expect?

I couldn't schedule the time she would be euthanized during that conversation, because I couldn't wrap my mind around it. Rondy was part of our family, and I felt like I was betraying her by even having the conversation.

As the months passed, Rondy's health progressively declined to the point I had to schedule the appointment. I remember the day I did; I bawled like a broken hearted school girl. The clerk at the veterinarian's office probably thought I was mentally unstable because I kept sniffling and choking up when I told her I needed to set an appointment to euthanize my dog.

But it was set. The date was set in stone, and Rondy would not suffer any longer.

On the morning of "the day," we gathered all the children in the family room to say goodbye to Rondy. Ryan was in first grade so he would be off to school, and Jenna and Maggie were going off for a play date for the day.

We didn't tell them what was happening other than they needed to give Rondy a special hug and tell her that they loved her. In some ways, looking back, I wish we had been clearer, but I didn't think little minds could handle it. Plus, I didn't want my children thinking that when a dog, or more importantly dad, gets old and loses control of his bodily functions the only recourse is to be put down.

On that cold December morning, after the kids were gone, it was just Rondy and me in the house. I said my goodbyes.

I cried, and I cried.

You see, I love dogs. I can't stand cats, but I love dogs. And I loved *this* dog because Rondy had been a part of our family from the beginning.

As the clock ticked closer to the time, I gathered Rondy into my arms and carried her to the garage and placed here in the back of my Pontiac Aztec where she laid down immediately to rest.

I got into the car, and the radio was tuned to our radio station that plays gospel music. Every song was about death.

First, there was:

*When I've gone the last mile of the way,*
*I will rest at the close of the day;*
*And I know there are joys that await me,*
*When I've gone the last mile of the way.*

This song was followed up by:

*When I come to the river at the ending of day*
*When the last winds of sorrow have blown*
*There'll be somebody waiting to show me the way*
*I won't have to cross Jordan alone*

I was so depressed I changed the station to a country station playing "Pain, Despair, and Agony on Me." That *really* cheered me up.

Finally, we arrived at the vet's office, and I carried Rondy into a private exam room. The vet came in and explained what would happen and said she would give me some time with the dog.

I sat there on the floor petting my puppy, again misty-eyed and wondered if I was crueler by taking her life or more selfish if I called it off to make her suffer.

Before I could come to a conclusion, the vet came and asked if I was ready, and I said I was. She reached over and gently petted Rondy and then gently placed a needle into the dog's neck and inserted the medicine.

Rondy's body was between my legs as we lay on the floor, and her head was resting on my thigh. For about three minutes, I stroked her head as she looked up at me while she drifted off into eternity.

I was a mess! She died peacefully, but I was not at peace at all. It is never easy to say goodbye to anyone you love whether canine or human.

After about 20 minutes, the vet returned and asked what I would like to do with "the remains." They offered to take care of them, or I can take her home to bury her. I asked what they do, and they said they have a service that takes care of the remains. (I later found out it was a dumpster out behind the vet's office.)

I chose to take her home and give her a proper burial in our backyard so that our kids would have a place to mark her memory. I assumed they would have body bag of some type to place the remains in, but I was surprised to find they used a large garbage bag.

That broke my heart. Rondy deserved better than that, especially for what I paid.

So on a cold, dreary December afternoon, I was charged with the responsibility of burying an 80-pound dog before my children could come home—in about an hour.

The ground was frosted with snow and frozen from the subzero temperature that day, but I frantically drove my Aztec to the backyard and ran to the garage to get a shovel and hoe.

Feverishly and furiously, I dug a deep hole next to the oak tree in the backyard. As I was digging, I noticed our elderly neighbor lady, an Edith Kravitz type neighbor, watching my every move out her back window.

Finally, the grave was dug.

I climbed into the hatchback of my car and tried to maneuver Rondy's remains to bury her gracefully, but rigor mortis had set in.

I awkwardly lifted her stiffen body still in the plastic garbage bag up from the back of the hatch and unintentionally flung her into the grave. Exasperated, I looked up to see my neighbor's eyes bug out at the spectacle. I had no time to explain. My kids were coming home soon, so I hurriedly covered the grave and placed a marker on it for time and eternity.

Naturally, I forgot to go over to explain to my nosy neighbor what I had been doing and what had happened. I did notice she was at her window counting our kids to see if any were missing. But I think she figured it out…it took a while, but she figured it out.

That was in December. The following summer, Jenny and I were sitting on the back deck talking, when Ryan, Jenna, and Maggie interrupted us as they passed through. Ryan was 6 or 7 years old and was loosely carrying a large shovel over his shoulder.

Knowing this was probably something that was not good, I said, "What are you up to, Ryno?"

Without batting an eye, he said, "We're going to see Rondy."

"Huh?" I said surprised.

He said, "Jenna, Maggie and me miss Rondy, and we want to see her again."

At that point, I had to sit down and yet again explain the concept of death.

I did the whole spiel: the cycle of life, birth and death, and most importantly eternal life. But the point of this conversation was that dead things are buried and should remain undisturbed. Dead things have passed away.

As I said those words "passed away" to my kids, I remembered the Apostle Paul's words in 2 Corinthians 5:17.

> *"Therefore if any man be in Christ, he is a new creature: old things are*

*passed away; behold, all things are become new*."

It was one of those moments that God taught me what to do with the old man that was spiritually dead and passed away. Keep him buried.

I think we preachers and Bible teachers have so wonderfully preached on the newness of life found in Jesus Christ and His powerful salvation, but we have failed to teach about how practical sanctification is seen in keeping the "old things that have passed away" buried.

We are sometimes like my kids who miss the "old dog" from our past. Yes, she is dead. Yes, she is decomposing, but we want to dig her up and pet on her a little.

As ridiculous as the prospect is of digging up a dead dog may be, it is even more ridiculous to consider digging up the "old things that have passed away" buried by God. We are His new creation. We are raised to newness of life, and the old man is dead.

"Old things" is the Greek term *archaios*, from *arche,* meaning "the beginning." *Archaios* is used of Satan the "old serpent" [from the beginning] in Revelation 12:9.

Thomas Constable has an intriguing thought on what is new and what is old in believers:

> Obviously there is both continuity and discontinuity that takes place at conversion (justification). Paul was not denying the continuity. We still have the same physical features, basic personality, genetic constitution, parents, susceptibility to temptation (1Co 10:13), sinful environment (Gal 1:4), etc. These things do not change. He was stressing the elements of discontinuity: perspectives, prejudices, misconceptions, enslavements, etc. (cf. Gal 2:20). God adds many new things at conversion including new spiritual life, the Holy Spirit, forgiveness, the righteousness of Christ, as well as new viewpoints (2Co 5:16).[xiv]

Constable is strictly speaking about that which has been from the beginning—the old Adamic nature. We were physically born with it, and before God can regenerate us to newness of life, there must be a funeral and burial for the "old man."

"Passed away" is in the aorist tense and indicative mood which indicates this passing away as an actual (real) historical event in the life of every believer. When did this occur in your life history? The instant that you confessed Jesus as

Lord (Romans 10:9, 10) and received Him as Savior, all by grace through faith (Ephesians 2:8, 9), you were born-again (John 3:3-8) and were irreversibly transferred from the kingdom of darkness into the kingdom of light, the kingdom of God's beloved Son (Colossians 1:13; Acts 26:18). At that glorious, miraculous moment in eternity, the "old you" ceased to exist in God's eyes, and henceforth and forever and ever, He views you as "in Christ."

Praise God for the funeral of the old man and the birth of the new creation!

That begs the question: why do we get the shovel to dig up old habits, hurts, and hang-ups that have been buried by God?

The best story I've heard of being a "new creation" and the buried "old man" is of Augustine. In his younger years, he had indulged in great sins. After his conversion, he met a woman who had been the sharer of his wicked promiscuity. She had approached him enticingly and said to him, "Augustine," but he ran away from her with all speed. She called after him, "Augustine it is I."

He turned around and said, "But it is not I. The old Augustine is dead, and I am a new creature in Christ Jesus!"

So, child of God, your Father is teaching you today to put down the shovel and stop digging up the past. You are a new creation in Christ; old things have "passed away."

# CHAPTER TEN

# *Importunity*

Importunity.

That's not a word you often hear in the ordinary conversation of daily life. While a bit arcane in use, the word is powerful in meaning. The Merriam-Webster Dictionary defines it as "urgent or persistent in solicitation, sometimes annoyingly so."

The most widely known use is found in Luke 11:8 in the story of the neighbor seeking, begging, and continually asking for bread from another neighbor at the most inconvenient time of midnight. It is in that context that Jesus makes the application about our prayer life.

*And I say unto you, Ask, and it shall be given you; seek, and ye shall find; knock, and it shall be opened unto you. – Luke 11:9*

Each of the verbs, ask, seek, and knock, lends itself to the idea of *continual* action…asking, seeking, and knocking. Thus the term importunity.

As a reasonable, intelligent person, I find it hard to consider the quality of importunity as part of my prayer life. But Jesus not only commended importunity but commanded it as a means to touch our Father's heart.

I must admit that my children's importunity has often touched my heart. The most recent illustration is my youngest son's, Josiah's, pleas for a puppy.

I'll have admitted I am a dog lover. I have no use for cats, but that is another story. Dogs I love. It took me a long time to recover from Rondy's passing to the point I had issued a decree that would never be another dog in the Lands' house. But my decree was no match for Josiah's determination.

I was out of town when my cell phone rang, and I heard Josiah's timid voice. "Daddy, can we get a puppy?"

There was no "Hello…how are you doing? Or "…are you busy? Just, "Daddy, can we get a puppy?"

Thus began the importunity. I confess I missed having man's best friend in our home. Before you judge and tell me that a man's best friend is his wife, let me challenge you to take a dog and your wife and lock them in a closet for an hour, and see which one comes out wagging their tail, happy to see you. That's a joke—don't *really* try that. But you see my point of how a dog loves unconditionally. That's why they are man's best friend.

Josiah knew where my heart was, but I had been reticent to bring another dog into our home because of the heartbreak of euthanizing our previous dog. But Josiah was importunate.

Not only did he have a request for a puppy, but for a *specific* puppy, he had found on the local Humane Society web page. Yes, my seven-year-old son researched before he requested a puppy, and picked his dog—Roscoe.

Then came the barrage of texts (when he would get hold of his mother's phone) and emails with pictures of the dog he wanted.

I admit, the first time I saw that nervous little lemon beagle's picture, my heart melted. Not so much because of the dog, but that my son had thoughtfully chosen him out of the 150 dogs on the website.

My phone kept ringing with texts like a Salvation Army kettle bell ringer, and my email was full of reasons why we need a dog. It got to a point where I was hesitant to call home because it tore me up to hear my little boy's pitiful voice asking for the puppy.

Finally, when I arrived home on Friday night, Jenny had told Josiah he had better back off on the begging, which he did, but when I saw him, his eyes said more than his mouth. When I tucked him in bed, he broke my heart when he told he had been praying that no one would take "Roscoe" until I had a chance to go visit him.

I told Jenny that we would sneak down to the pound and at least look. Josiah's importunity was answered as he knew that was all it would take.

The next morning, Jenny and I went out for our regular Saturday morning breakfast date and then stopped by the pound. The attendants walked us through the cages of dogs and cats until we came outside to the shelter cage where little Roscoe was kept.

He sat there on his hind legs shivering and whimpering with glistening big brown eyes as if to say, "Take me home." The attendant opened the cage, and I picked Roscoe up, and he nuzzled his head under my chin.

That's all it took. I carried that puppy home in my arms and welcomed him into his new family. The first time Josiah held Roscoe was a particular moment I will never forget. I will never regret yielding to my son's importunity because my heart was already there with his.

I believe that is what Jesus is teaching us about prayer. We can keep asking and seeking when we know that what is on our heart is also on our Father's heart. It isn't the relentless nagging of a spoiled child that our Father gives into, but the heart of God that is touched by the genuine heartfelt pleas of a child.

Why was my heart so close to Josiah's heart? Because he is my son. He is the spitting image of me physically and in personality. I have no science to prove it, but there is a gene in both of us for love of dogs.

My point is this: when you come to your Heavenly Father and ask for things that are genuinely on your heart, placed there within the divine nature you have as His child, you will have His attention.

So don't stop asking. Don't quit knocking. Never cease from seeking. Don't give up on the burdens on your heart but keep praying with a spirit of importunity to your Father who shares your heart.

# CHAPTER ELEVEN
## *I Can't Even Walk*

"Rub my feet, Daddy."

I hear that quite a bit from my little princess. Late in the evening, she comes to lay on mine and Jenny's bed to talk to us and to get a foot rub. I wish I could say I always oblige. Unfortunately, I don't. But when I do, I'm reminded of Jenna's need for a compassionate touch.

To understand Jenna's request, you need some context. This story begins all the way back in April of 2004. Jenny was great with children, particularly with our twin girls.

Their birth had been a soap opera of early contractions and magnesium infusions to stop the labor for about three months. But now the time had come, and the doctor was going to perform a

Caesarean section on Jenny to welcome our little girls to the world.

You can imagine our anticipation. We had seen our girls via ultrasound, even the earliest renditions of the three-dimensional ultrasound. But honestly, you have to use your imagination to be able to see anything through that cloudy image.

I was all dressed up like a surgeon and escorted to the operating room. There I sat at the end of the table where Jenny's head had been partitioned off from her distended, pregnant belly. She couldn't feel a thing but fear and excitement. I was numb myself.

I will spare you all the gory details. It was pretty much a textbook delivery via c-section with each daughter delivered two minutes apart. I cut the cords, and the babies were immediately taken aside to get their APGAR scores.

They didn't cry so much as they squeaked. But the girls' lungs were open, and they were breathing.

Then I saw the nurses gather around Jenna, still being referred to as Baby One. One nurse said, "It looks like Baby One has Talipes Equinovarus."

A look of horror came across Jenny's face, and in my mind, I said, "Talipes Equino-what is?"

The doctor asked, "Did the ultrasound show any congenital disabilities?"

Now my mind raced, and Jenny began weeping.

"No," I choked out.

"Well, Baby One has dual club feet."

I popped my head up above the partition, and there I saw Jenna as they were cleaning her up. Her feet were turned in like an "L" and a "J," and she was kicking them hard.

We learned that it was positional Talipes Equinovarus because the girls ran out of room in the womb.

Thus began a lengthy process of casts and surgeries for my princess. They immediately placed casts on her feet to start the process of proper formation.

I remember when they had to bend her ankles to get her feet in proper position to cast her, and she began screaming a deathly scream.

Jenny and I both wept as the doctor did it. That was my little girl, and I know it had to be done, but I didn't want it to be so painful.

In her earliest baby portrait, you can see pink casts peeking out from under her frilly pink dress.

Fast forward to the crawling years. Those casts slowed Jenna down, but they didn't stop her. She would crawl everywhere, because she had within her resilience, a toughness, which only this handicap could form.

Once Jenny and I were walking through the area around Entebbe Fountain in Rome, Italy. This area is notorious for pick-pockets and beggars. But while there, we saw a little boy on a mechanic's creeper with two grossly deformed club feet.

He appeared to be the same age as Jenna.

This poor boy didn't have the medical care we were able to give Jenna, and because of that, he was consigned to pushing himself around the bumpy paths of Old Rome on a worn-out mechanic's creeper.

I gave the kid everything I had in my pocket. Maybe I shouldn't have, but in my mind, I had to do something.

Looking back, I realize Jenny and I did the same thing for our Jenna. We gave her everything we could, and as hard as it was, it was needed.

It was agony to hear her scream during her castings or at therapy or after her surgeries. But it was necessary.

We would not have been loving parents if we hadn't let her go through some temporary pain to be able to walk normally. It was worth it to see her run up and down the soccer field and the basketball court today. It will be worth it when I walk her down the aisle to present her to her Prince Charming.

It wasn't easy, but it was necessary.

The Apostle Paul wrote, "For our light affliction, which is but for a moment, worketh for us a far more exceeding and eternal weight of glory" (2 Corinthians 4:17). What we are facing now is light compared to the eternal blessing that is ahead.

Our Heavenly Father knows that eliminating temporal pain in correcting and healing the birth defect of sin in our lives isn't good for the long run. He is allowing us to be formed and strengthened for the future. He is preparing us for eternity.

One day, we will be walked down a celestial aisle and be presented as a perfect Bride.

> *That he might present it to himself a glorious church, not having spot, or wrinkle, or any such thing; but that it should be holy and without blemish.*
> *– Ephesians 5:27*

So today, lean on your Father as you walk the path before you. It will be worth it.

*Lord, I can't even walk without you holding my hand*
*The mountains too high and the valleys too wide*
*Down on my knees, that's where I learned to stand*
*Lord; I can't even walk without you holding my hand.*[xv]

# C O N C L U S I O N

As I grow older and value more the fleeting, mundane moments in life, I recognize how much I've been taught through my children—or, more specifically, by raising my children.

Through being a parent, I've discovered the rhythm of God's heartbeat. I've learned, although our Heavenly Father wants only the best for us, He won't force our hands to clutch it. I have free will, and so do my children. And when my kids decide to disobey and bear the consequences, I experienced some of our Lord's sorrow when He watches His children do the very same thing.

I am learning that what I am teaching the children points back to me directly and that my character is between God and me.

When God instructed Moses of the *Shema* in Deuteronomy 6:5, He declared:

> *And thou shalt teach them diligently unto thy children, and shalt talk of them when thou sittest in thine house, and when thou walkest by the way, and when thou liest down, and when thou risest up.*
> – *Deuteronomy 6:7*

As parents, it is our responsibility to teach our children by *talking* and *walking.* But I have learned that in my speaking and walking with my children, it is through them that God has shown me and is still teaching me.

As of this writing, we are into the teenage years in the Lands' home. I question why teenagers think they are entitled. In frustration, I said to Jenny, "They should be thankful we provide for them, protect them, and are there for them. Why do they often have such an irrational sense of entitlement?"

Then in my bluster, God whispered into my ear again, "You sometimes feel like you too are entitled to a burden-free life and yet I provide for you and I am always here for you, and I love you."

I've discovered so much from my children about trusting God, myself and my parents.

In the last eighteen years of parenting, I have learned and am re-learning that my Heavenly Father is always right, even when what is happening in my life seems wrong. His heart is broken when I cry out to Him. He is still good when circumstances are bad. He always loves, even though He may seem silent.

These are the lessons I am learning about my Heavenly Father with my children as my teachers.

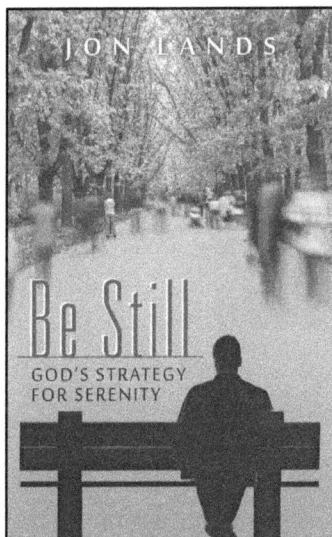

JON LANDS

Be Still
GOD'S STRATEGY
FOR SERENITY

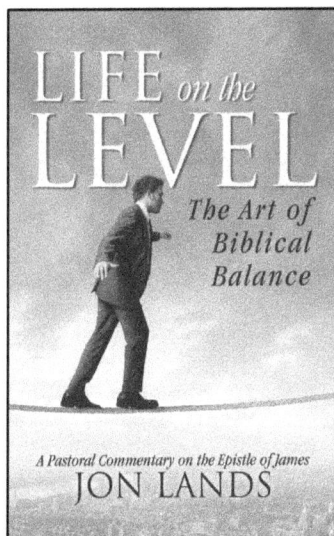

LIFE on the
LEVEL
The Art of
Biblical
Balance

A Pastoral Commentary on the Epistle of James
JON LANDS

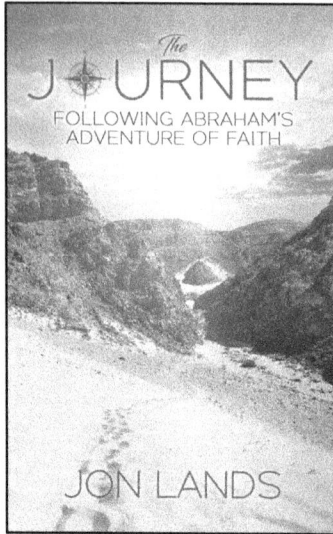

*The*
J✦URNEY
FOLLOWING ABRAHAM'S
ADVENTURE OF FAITH

JON LANDS

*Available at Amazon, Barnes & Noble*
*and other fine booksellers.*
*Also online at*
*www.TheWordForLifeRadio.com*

# ENDNOTES

[i] https://boardofwisdom.com/togo/Quotes/ShowQuote?msgid=935 69#.WfUDDo9Sxdg (Sourced: 10/14/17)

[ii] http://www.faithgateway.com/what-was-meant-for-evil-god-uses-for-good/#.VAYc4WN_SLw (Sourced: 10/14/17)

[iii] Dyer, Judy Cantrell (2013), CreateSpace Independent Publishing Platform.

[iv] https://www.messie2vie.fr/bible/strongs/strong-hebrew-H0750-arek.html (Sourced: 12/10/17)

[v] Hamilton, V. P. (1999). 162 אָרַךְ. In R. L. Harris, G. L. Archer, Jr. & B. K. Waltke (Eds.), Theological Wordbook of the Old Testament (R. L. Harris, G. L. Archer, Jr. & B. K. Waltke, Ed.) (electronic ed.) (72). Chicago: Moody Press.

[vi] Tan, P. L. (1996). Encyclopedia of 7700 Illustrations: Signs of the Times (1069). Garland, TX: Bible Communications, Inc.

[vii] Bush, Laura (2010), *Spoken from the Heart,* Simon and Schuster, page 24.

[viii] Pink, Arthur W. (2001) A. W. Pink's Studies in the Scriptures, Volume 8, Sovereign Grace Publishers.

[ix] Dobson, James. *The New Strong Willed Child,* Tyndale House Publishers, Inc., 2017, page 37.

[x] Edwards, Jonathan. *The Freedom of Will,* Courier Corporation, 2012, pages 183-184.

[xi] Dobson, page 62.

[xii] http://www.dictionary.com/browse/parenting?s=t (Sourced = 7/12/2016)

[xiii] A Manifesto Against 'parenting' – Wall Street Journal https://www.wsj.com/articles/a-manifesto-against-parenting-1467991745) (Sourced = 4/20/17)

[xiv] http://www.soniclight.com/constable/notes/pdf/2corinthians.pdf (Sourced = 7/11/17)

[xv] Craft, Colbert and Joyce, "I Can't Even Walk Without You Holding My Hand", 1974.

www.ingramcontent.com/pod-product-compliance
Lightning Source LLC
Chambersburg PA
CBHW031601040426
42452CB00006B/371